About the Author

Writing has always been Sally Rawhey's passion. She has worked her way through different types of writing, from journalism, magazine editing, television programs, script writing, ads, copywriting to song lyrics and documentaries' script writing. For over a decade, Sally Rawhey worked as a Television Programs Director and Creative Director in different television channels in the Middle East.

However, it has always been the magic of writing that moved her and the symphony that a well-written poem creates. In her book, *The Unspoken Voices*, Sally Rawhey reveals in her collection of poems the feelings of many silent hearts that are flooded with love in its many magical forms.

THE UNSPOKEN VOICES

SALLY RAWHEY

THE UNSPOKEN VOICES

Olympia Publishers
London

www.olympiapublishers.com
OLYMPIA PAPERBACK EDITION

A CIP catalogue record for this title is
available from the British Library.

ISBN: 978-1-78830-236-4

First Published in 2018
Olympia Publishers
60 Cannon Street
London
EC4N 6NP

Printed in Great Britain

Dedication

"HE", the Creator of Love... my heart floods with rivers of YOUR love.

"Him", Dad... who planted this dream inside me, for you I bloom.

"Her", Mum... my universe lies inside your eyes, it's only there I can survive.

"Thee", Brother... the loving back that forever shielded me from the winds.

"The One", My Beloved Husband... I will love you as long as I live.

"She", Nuts... happiness is an hour with you.

"Them", My Kids... The reason for my life is the gift of you.

A Sin Called Love

Have I sinned
when I longed for you;
when I closed my eyes
and saw but you?

Have I sinned
to happily smile,
following my heartbeats
mile after mile?

Have I sinned
to speak unheard,
my love like angels
worshipping God?

Have I sinned
to feel warmth
of your hand on mine,
when we never touched?

Have I sinned?
I have no strength
to drown feelings,
they float right back.

Have I sinned
to think of you
morning and night?
Am I destroying everything that's right?

Have I sinned
when I loved?
Do they jail or slaughter
victims of love?

The world says yes but
your eyes say no;
heart pleads to stay,
mind pleads, go.

I'm lost in between
feelings and fears,
smiles and tears,
your warmth and your spears

Is there a way out
when steps move in,
walking to you,
away from you?

Adoring you so
hating you more,
wanting you to stay
leaving you once more.

Forgive me,
if I have sinned.
Love is my punishment,
loving against my will.

Worst Happiness

In which you said I'd come
then left,
Stripped my dreams off
In a brutal theft,
In which I laughed away the tears
And carved my passion into spears,
In which I stabbed that very heart
that fell for you from the start.
In which tomorrow is another tomorrow
Free of you and free of your sorrow.

What Aged Your Heart?

Why do shadows shade the heart
Was it unfairness that tore it apart
Or was it a love that chose to depart,
Tell me, was it ever soft from the start?
What made the senses wilt,
Was it the years or was it the guilt.
Did it turn into stone,
From their deeds or your own?
Do we truly grow harsh with time,
Become like coarse meat or stale wine
Or are we unjustly blaming time?
A black heart is born blind,
It's not the age,
It's the darkness of the mind.

We are only the colors we chose,
Who chooses light,
Will grow a heart of white.
One that sees beauty,
In the darkest night.
One that jumps like a child,
Regardless of who's in sight.
A dreamer has a heart that never grows,
No wrinkles will ever carve his brows.

Youth will always shine behind
The white hair and forgetful mind.
For age is weak before a dream,
Its tranquility lasts like a flowing stream
Of fresh water clear and pure.
He who has a good soul
Will not age for sure.
For every illness of the heart,
He has a cure.

London in Vain

Stop it, London
don't twist and turn
the cold rain, the sharp stern
an old lady selling you wine
calling you "darling" a dozen times
the blue eyes, the pale skin.
Oh, London, like your heavy clouds
a mere product of sin.
Victoria is her name
another station different yet the same
one vicious like King's town
one lustful like Piccadilly's
music playing everywhere
by young hungry bellies
waiting for a dime
from your hand or mine
before you squeeze in and push
oh Lord, an empty seat to Shepherd's Bush!

You have to be lucky
Like is a game of hockey
the "faster" will win,
don't look out for your kin
take the left side of the escalators and sprint.

If hungry, chew that British mint
Life in London is tough
Even the air you breathe is expensive stuff
Skip Lola's cupcakes
Don't waste that five pounds
On Prêt à Manger
You're not a Parisian
"Qui peut payer?"
Don't sulk and whine
Walk the Hyde Park, feed a swan
Pretend you're that rich guy in Harrods
All comes true with a little win.

Stop it London
Don't twist and turn
lovers have escaped you
their dreams here did burn.
"*Mamma Mia*" says it in its fancy musical
How "*Thriller*" can be rough
Yet utterly magical.
And down the lane of Bond Street
The paella called me
I gave up Shake Shack's treat
A frenzy of taste
expensive food not a bite to waste.
You stroll along
Taken by the rain
Attempts of befriending London
die all in vain
and there, inside its gates

a place ageless, unbothered by dates
Covent Garden, a garden with no garden
a treatment for those whose senses did harden
all sparkly and tidy
like a middle-aged woman
looking twenty and speaking ninety.

Stop it London
Don't shift and turn
I am a stranger in love
don't turn me to stone,
I've roamed your streets passionately
I've fallen in love on my own
with London the villain
the kingdom that conquered Rome.
The gardens of Buckingham
The Voxcyl Dam
The Tea House Theatre cake
The open-mic poetry where nothing's fake
I've walked past it all
with one target and one goal
to unclose the roots of your arrogance
that made you pursued by all.

Just Me On Earth

Someone was behind me
following me, tracking me, chasing me.
it was a moonless night
heavy rain was blurring my sight
there were no crowds, no families, no lovers holding tight,
no cars, no machines, no products of any worth
No trace of humanity on the face of earth
No other breath, no other face
except for footsteps that followed my every pace.
I raced faster down the muddy street,
My heart sinking with every beat.
From street to street I ran,
with no target, no plan,
just a little voice inside me predicting danger,
and a secret hidden with the stranger.

Suddenly out of nowhere appeared a train
It was beautiful but shady
like it dropped out of ancient Spain.
Once the wheels started moving,
I was imprisoned in a compartment without a soul,
not even a driver to take his role.
Just the engine and I traveling through empty space.
I searched for any passenger,

but there was not a single face.
I smashed the windows and waited for blood to fall,
but nothing came out
except the courage that ruled my soul.
I jumped out to a crowded street,
full of people and strange music.
They were different,
their faces human, yet inhuman.
Their voices like echoes from my past,
their smiles like children,
their sounds like angels.
Perhaps they were aliens
or maybe, I was the alien.

Everything was so confusing
My mind had no peace.
It felt like I had lived another lifetime
and their faces were a mere reflection of my face.
I reached out to touch them but I couldn't feel,
the whole scene was so unreal.
They were far and close at the same time
Like enemies yet partners in crime
I felt them call out to me
but my voice did not get through,
some invisible wall was blocking me too.
There were no footsteps
and for a moment I envied my chaser,
who must have found a lover
while I remained a stranger.
I flew away, indifferent to their echoes,
fleeing from their world that refused to admit me.

The footsteps returned again
Following me down the streets
and back to—emptiness?
I don't know how long I ran,
months or years.
I don't know how far I reached
mountains or streams?
I don't know why I was being chased
or who was chasing me?
Enemy or ally,
devil or angel,
friend or foe,
dream or reality,
past or future—
a stranger or just me?
I had no strength to think or strive,
my mind doubted I was still alive.
Everything was so vague before me
All was unknown but my invisible chaser
As tightly close as a cardiac pacer
The only proof of my existence,
my sole companion to this sentence.

He and I were mates
In a history that erased its dates.
I stopped, it was time to face the stranger,
I couldn't run any more from the danger
I waited but I couldn't hear,
I turned 'cause I was wild with fear,
for it had come to be with me when

none existed to be with me again.
It was a young woman,
dressed in my clothes
smiling my smile
I did not need to ask her who she was.
I saw the answer in my eyes,
heard it in my breath,
felt it in my smile.
The mirror was clear then,
the fog was fading away
I was free to go
and I was free to stay.

Mother in Wrong

I am your mother
and I am all wrong,
teach me in moments of fear
to stay strong,
and not shed a tear.

I am your mother
and I am all wrong
I care too much,
I worry too much,
I try to sway any danger
far from your touch.

I am your mother
and I am all wrong.
I cry when I shouldn't,
I flare up when I shouldn't,
If love is my excuse
I'm guilty as accused.
I'll let go,
I promise I will.

This Beautiful Person
I can never strip off its will,

This special smile
I can never kill.
I will chain this heart
that yearns to protect you.
My will won't grow into a danger
that judges and attacks you.

I am your mother
and I am all wrong
I promise I won't hurt you
with a love so ill,
for your happiness
I'll do anything and everything
I promise you—I will.

Hit the Ground

What brings you here
my silly mind?
What made you willingly
fall behind?
Why love a heart
created blind?

You dared later, sat and whined!
What dragged you in?
What were you expecting to find?
Empty vessels always
make the loudest sound.
You should have known better
You shouldn't have been kind.

A wrong love will kill you;
it will tear and grind.
It will strip you of yourself
You'll eventually hit the ground.
And you were not born a slave,
walk away, don't look behind!

Loose Chains

If fish were given wings, would they fly?
If birds grew fins, would they swim?
Would snails cease to crawl if they had legs?
If silence was given lips,
would it speak out?
If we were given freedom would we ever feel free?
We feel it, we dream of it, we speak of it,
but we dare not live it.
Just like a long line of ants we move,
none of us daring to step out of line.
The tracks before us are the only ones we follow,
even if they end in hell.

Just like a mad man can't give away his madness for peace
of mind
or a clown can't wear a sad face after living on giggles,
we can't.
Just like a widowed woman can't wish back her dead
husband
or a lonely orphan can't experience a single, motherly hug,
we can't.
We can't learn to try in an age that breaks every promise.
Our eyes won't dare to gaze into each other's eyes.

Curtains of blame will fall down and blind them,
our words will never be heard,
we'll always have to whisper.
Our hands will never touch.
The whole world will come in between.

We were born with these chains,
fed and nurtured till they fit us perfectly.
Taught that love is beautiful
only when it beautifies the real intentions.
The lesson was loud and clear:
"Love only the blooming roses"
but if we turn to admire the cactus
the whole world stands alarmed,
warning and blaming us
for favoring what the world demeaned.

And years sweep by with silent regrets
that pass unnoticed like growing cactus.
We dream of growing a hundred legs
to run faster than the whole world,
to walk in when all others walk out.
We long to speak feelings out loud,
without shame, without blame.
We try to destroy our chains,
but we usually fail.
Perhaps because we ask the world for freedom,
when we need it from ourselves?

You can liberate prisoners,

you can liberate countries.
You can free birds from their cages
and relieve the body from pain
but you can't take away the waves from the oceans
and the wind from the skies,
you can't free feelings
they lie under loose chains.

Laugh Out Loud

Laugh, laugh so loud
let the sand in the waves color your hair
the color of the clouds.
Let your voice ring all about
give in to joy and never doubt.
Come, sprinkle your dreams with ice cream,
Come, whistle along,
sing or even scream.
Come, let's draw happy faces with whipped cream,
Flip and turn all the rules they set around,
leave no borders,
cross every ground.
Stick out your tongue,
don't let fear utter a single sound.

Laugh, laugh so loud
I know your game and I can dance too,
I will hop, I will rock, I will salsa with you,
laugh, laugh so loud.
Don't stare at the crowd,
the heart is but a child born wild.
Laugh, laugh so loud.
Throw sand in the air
make soap bubbles everywhere,

sink your face in the cold sea,
come scribble on the sand with me.
Roll up your pants and let's race the tide.
God created nothing purer than a child
so why captivate a heart,
born to be wild?

Beast of an Angel

She has a heart of shimmering gold.
She laughs, she sweet talks, she hardly grows old.
She takes risks, she's naturally bold.
The warmth in her eyes melts hearts naturally cold.
They say she's like an angel,
but don't believe everything told.

If you step on her love
you're cursed from above.
No canines are needed,
no wilder beast was ever created
you'll be finished in a sec
a heart that stabs her is better dead!

It's Eternal

Hate love as much as you want
call it an illness of the heart,
put off any sparkle from its start
love will rekindle its glow,
when you least expect it so.
Love is a foe you can't overthrow,
'cause it's eternal.

Shatter love into pieces,
and scatter it between cities,
burn it into charcoal,
and bury it in the deepest hole,
cross it out of existence
refuse it with instance
it will follow you from a distance,
'cause it's eternal.

Make the people demean it
look down on it,
loathe it and defeat it,
you still can't beat it,
'cause it's eternal.

Call out your armies,
slaughter all love's memories,
let them wilt like autumn leaves,
its flowers will still bloom,
from the windows of your own room
it will grow in spite of the gloom,
just like babies in a womb,
'cause it's eternal.

Shield your heart with steel boards,
grab your sharpest swords
and forbid any lovely words
just like free-flying souls,
you can't captivate love behind walls,
'cause it's eternal.

Tell Him You're There

The sea crashes loudly with magnificent waves
then seeps softly with tiny ripples,
to say it.
The air blows its wind to hurricanes
then exchanges it with the softest breeze,
to say it.
The trees cover up their leaves with countless fruits
then shed their branches bare,
to say it.
The skies display infinite shining stars
then conceal them with a few passing clouds,
to say it.
Yet the heart,
the greatest of His creations
may pass a lifetime
without saying it.

Alive For Five Days

Listen to my story
of days that were so long and slow
of a girl who is me.
A girl younger than the years she lived
A girl who thought of innocence as a virtue,
but life mocked the child in her eyes.
A girl who thought she knew of love so well
and painted her dreams and papers with it,
a girl who shyly tried to catch the glow of love in the eyes
of lovers,
for its shine gave her a reason to be.
A girl who believed that God hides her rivers of love
under closed eyelids so the world cannot see.
Listen well now
the story begins. It begins at an end.

At the time when hands are just about to shake goodbye,
when my eyes will no more see your eyes,
when backs will turn and move away.
Where "gone" will be the word I use
when my heart asks, "Where is he?"
At this very ending,
my story begins.
It begins with a count-down.

They placed all the clocks of the world before me,
marked their watches to the minutes and the seconds
then they opened the doors of heaven
to let me walk into you.

The moon suddenly turned brighter than the seven suns,
the summer's heat became like a breeze ever so sweet.
The silence grew hands and played the most beautiful
songs,
the long boring hours came and left like they never came.
I changed into a painter,
a singer, a bird,
a butterfly, a flying kite.
I shift and change into the colors of the rainbow
our faces don't smile as the whole world watches,
why do we have to paint our faces with smiles
when the soul is dancing with happiness?
Why do we have to speak?
When in spite of the walls in between
I hear your voice coming through.

Why do we have to see?
The eyes go blind with sleep
but the heart can still see.
I see you, I feel you, I hear you,
I am you.
Or are you a dream I invented in a moment of loneliness
when the heart was weeping with pain?
Or are you a truth that I can't possess,
yet can't resist.

Are you mine or am I just to watch you from far?
I am lost in your world
on the clouds that you drew with your words,
like birds sent from heaven to make me human
heal me from the frozen shell I hid behind,
they gave me wings, I can fly, I can fly.

You made me discover something so important.
I discovered I'm alive. I breathe. I feel—I am me.
I have a voice that sounds like an angel when it calls your
name.
The voice does not come from my lips but deep inside me.
I discovered that I am alive. Alive—for five days.
Then the curtains will fall on this story
and the living me will walk to the frozen me,
to that very same little, rusted shell
you found me hiding inside.

He

And He whispers, "Come close,"
but the waves are rocking your seas so loud.
He blows the wind to carry you to His path,
but you only reach out to untangle the windblown hair.
He sends shining stars to grab your sight,
but all you see is the reflection of light on people's faces.
He places little stones before your feet to halt you,
but you childishly jump above them and go.
HE calls your name out loud
so that you may feel Him near before you sleep,
but you shut down your eyes and soul.
And yet HE whispers again,
He sends more shining stars,
He protects you, He heals you, He feels you,
again and again.
Forgive us,
Our sins have outnumbered the leaves of His trees,
But He promised to erase them,
Even if they outnumber the waves of the seas.

I Am But One

Don't follow in my footsteps
Even if the path had grace
Age did not add wisdom
Just lines on my face
I'm no one special in God's kingdom
I'm but one of this immortal race.

Forgive

I felt YOU moving away
I guess I was not worth YOUR stay.
I did all that I promised not to do
I disregarded my promise to YOU.
I walked to where You told me to stay off,
I longed for what you forbid and my heart sought
what it shouldn't seek.
I know the heart has its own will
but you warned from how it could fall ill.
And seek a past dream lying there still
I wish there was a way to kill
but it surfaces up,
I swear, against my will!
Lead me back into forgiveness.
YOU never are scarce with what you give
It's only with YOUR mercy that we live.
I beg YOU to add me among the sinners
YOU chose to forgive.

Lady in White

I'll wear white, only white can be worn on a day like this
the day birds are let out of their cages and allowed to
conquer the skies
the day orphans stop weeping for a minute to experience
the taste of smiles
the day ice is robbed of its coldness
and dreams enchant the soul like siren cries.
The day that knows no words of blame, shame or pain
the day the flag of love penetrates the lands
after centuries of exile,
the day my existence is announced to you.

You never knew I was the sun that touched your cheeks
every morning,
the water that washed your hands before your prayers,
the laugh of a child that made you smile,
the book that rests under your sleepy eyes every night
the strings that bring out heavenly tunes
from the touch of your hand
the eyes of every woman you loved.
I was there and you were everything,
the friend and the enemy,
the prince and the monster,
the man and the baby,
the night and the day,

the truth and the lie.

You were like a heavenly juice
that everyone longed to taste
and you never said no.
How many have you loved before my very eyes?
How many have you wept your nights for
and shared your mornings with?
How many have you drawn in your paintings
imagined their faces as you sang your love songs?
How many have you loved as I stood there watching you?

I've known each and every one of them.
I wrote their names down night after night.
I watched the redhead girls
to learn from the golden in their hair the way to your heart,
I gazed at the black-eyed girls
to understand from the movement of their lashes
the language of the eyes,
I studied their movements
their words, their lies
that I would find a place before them
to the secret tunnel where your heart lies.
Then I would try to go to you,
dressed up in your favorite colors
wearing your favorite smile
singing your warmest tunes
skin familiar with your every interest
that you may see love in me.

I left the world in search of you
I have climbed mountains and sailed the seas.
I have talked to the fog and questioned the echo about you.
I watched birds fly
that in the fluff of their wings I'd see you.
I listened to silence
that in its muteness I'd hear you through.
I drew many pictures
I wrote hundreds of poems
that in the mixture of colors and words,
you'd come true.
But something beyond my control
would take me elsewhere,
a power that forced my legs to move in the direction
opposite to you.

I would find myself walking back to my own room
carrying my dreams and fears in one bag
to watch the young heart of mine
age before my eyes.
The power that knew that you and I are like night and day,
eternally separated,
that being with you was against all the laws of reality
that life has created,
that finding love in your heart
was like searching for water in barren lands,
never irrigated.
But today is different.

Today all the ships are taking off from your harbors,
the winds are blowing the pages of your life in the air,
the little fish are swimming away from your shores
and eagles are flying high above your skies.
The stars are not counting you amongst them
and the waves are not waiting for your body to warm the
ocean.
Your taste has turned stale.
No one longs for it but I.
No woman will come looking for you again.
I will be your only route.
No woman but I can be your suit.

The shine of your eyes will be mine to cherish all alone.
Should I be happy or sad,
should I be laughing or mourning?
As I stare out at a world
that lost all the shades of colors
but white, just white tonight.
A white dress, a white room,
a white face, a white smile.

I walked out to you
as the sun threw its first baby ray
into the arms of the night.
In my hands every letter that has your name.
On my lips every tune you sang to the women you adored.
In my eyes all the feelings I hid from your stare
to place all my life before your dust.

It is a different life I can offer you now,
a life where eternal silence is the first and only language
we share,
where jealousy is from the worthless dust
not the beautiful women any more.

I have become like a sailor
who for years stood on a crowded harbor
watching ship after ship sail
until nothing remained but loose ropes
questioning the presence of a life ever on these waters.
I have become like a woman who lived all her life
longing to get pregnant,
then after months of pain
found before her a piece of unmoving flesh.

My heart has frozen from dreaming of warmth,
my lips have wilted from their unspoken words,
my body has shrunk from all this cold world.
Open your eyes.
Look now, it's me.
I am finally here.
Please look at me.
Look at the green of my eyes
and the golden strands of my hair
look at the honest feelings in my voice
and the innocent, pureness of my love
look well now
at the woman you never knew.

Beneath The Dream

Let me tell you a story
of a man I know so well.
You will not find him at the café
nor if you ring his bell.
If you're searching for the real him
I'll tell you if you will,
you might then meet him,
but find him
only few will.

Now follow me to this world
That has no time or space,
where nature is your gate
and beauty is in a race.
Look under the fallen leaves
or climb this hill of shells.
He hides beneath a dream,
but which, I cannot tell.

Where he hides is a secret
that only beauty will spell.
I've seen him painting a morning
from the shining starts at night.
I've felt him in soft candles burning

when music dances to the light.
I've watched him protect a wild dream
like his own baby, worth every fight.

I've wondered how he convinced beauty
to be his lifelong friend.
How is it that the two of them blend?
She gifts him with shadows
and he plants her roses of no end.

But where is he now?
Truth is, I couldn't tell.
Maybe under the shades of rainbow hides him still
or an old oak tree became his will.
Learn to search for simplicity
and you'll find him there.
You will.

Escape for Life

When the warm rays of the sun lose their way in the
frosting skies
and the first drops of rain frighten the stemming leaves,
winter arrives with its long, black nights.
All animals run for escape,
to the safe haven of a winter shelter.
But where do we humans go?
Where do we hide when the stingy cold reaches our souls
threatening the warmth in our hearts?
Where do we escape?
Some hold their loved ones to their sides,
watch in silence as the world disappears under snow.
While others just run alone like the presence of people
threatens their one chance of survival.

Very few of us stop to think that there could be a solution,
a way out of these freezing winds other than escape.
There are seasons for change.
Nature dictates and all creations obey.
But man, who values his days after they end
who picks up the fallen roses to gift them with water,
who sees no beauty but in a young face
who knows he is innocent yet pleads guilt.
Only man doesn't go by the rules of the game

there are no seasons for our hibernation
we hibernate for life in this world of silence.
The silence of lips when they lose their purpose
and give in to nothingness.

Hibernation became man's biggest habit,
his first resort when life scatters its thorns around him.
He becomes like the butterfly that seeks the comfort of its
cocoon,
the bear that disappears from the summer's heat,
the ostrich that digs its head in the sand when it falls prey.
Or perhaps more like man who hibernates in crisis
and appears after everything is gone.
We got so used to sleeping that we forgot how it feels to
be awake
Our eyes escaped the sharpness of black and white for so
long
it can't comprehend them any more,
reality became just another vague word in our dictionaries,
we replaced it with a more meaningful word to our state of
mind. Dreams.

And on these six letters we built our future,
raised our children and buried our loved ones.
A dream of countless wealth and a dream of touching
hands,
or dreams of success mingled with dreams of love,
dreams became our only entertainment in hibernation
our windows to the life we fear to face.
But were we created to run and keep on hiding?

Or have we been hibernating for so long
we forgot there could be a warm sun out there?
Winter is not the only season,
the cold is not the only enemy.
Passiveness is the sin
that we are human enough to sin.
Even animals don't escape for life.

I Loved

Tell the waves I loved,
tell it with every language and every dialect.
Tell the sea rocks, I too melted in the warmth more
forceful than joy dissolves in fears.
Tell the deep blue depths, I am colored with darker shades
than these waters can ever paint in years.
Tell these winds that roar, I too have flown in currents
stronger than the northern winds.
Tell this heavenly sea smell, I have smelt scents more
captivating than any tender breeze.
Tell this sparkling light, shine as you may, my eyes have
paired with a light unmatched and unseen.

Tell this body that stands tall above these waves, rocks
and seas, stand as long as you may, your traces will still be
washed away.
Tell this heart that synchronized its beats to your waves,
love and hate as you wish, only the good of your words
will remain.
Tell this kite that flies with your dreams beyond the
clouds, fly higher and higher, beyond this magical sea is a
far more beautiful bay.
Tell the sea I loved. Tell it with my voice, with my
heartbeat, with my breath, with my sight.

Tell it to HIM without fear, tell it without shedding a tear,
tell it if I remain or even if I disappear.
Tell HIM,
HE will listen. HE is forever near.

Inside Me

When my sick child turns and tells me, I have no pain,
I see YOU.
When in the middle of the worst fight and the anger
unexpectedly subsides,
I see YOU.
When lost and trembling with fear and I spot my haven
extremely near,
I see YOU.
YOU are not up high concealed by layers of skies,
Inside me, I see YOU.

No One

I saw how birds fly in the midst of fire,
how clouds shape up from nothingness
how anger builds along with laughter,
when feelings consume all
like serpents' poison.
I lived many days painted with tears,
the glitter of its wetness
taught me happiness.
I spoke silent words that still echo inside
a deserted island called the heart.
I gave so much of me
to no one
kept much more,
for no one.
I petted and laughed
with no one,
I felt and comforted
no one.
There was so much of me taken,
by no one.
And too much of me left
for no one.

I loved you, the non-existing,
just like you loved me, the untouchable.
I spared you myself,
and you gifted me yourself
for you and I
are no one.
Just a breeze that never blew
a sun that has no rays,
a river that can't sail boats
a flower that won't grow petals.
Who are you and who am I?
Who's the devil?
And who's the angel?
Who carries seeds of love,
in deserts of danger?
Who pleads desire
with the smile of an angel?
Like there is no beauty
but in sharing.

Who gives life a chance of fairness
in the middle of grief
and between strangers.
Who is right and who is not?
You claim you're an angel,
I dare you. "I am too."
You believe in the hero inside you,
and I proudly gaze at the one
deep in me too.
You see your fairness

but for me, only I am true.
But tell me,
how can life make virtue
a trait for me and you?

One of us is a liar
one of us is untrue.
It might be me
but what if it is you?
Will my heart take it?
Will I live it through?
And if you're wrong
what in life is worth
losing belief in you?
I don't want to lose
what I never had,
I don't want your image
to fade into blast,
I don't want to dissolve,
in a sea of no end.
For I have loved you,
the non-existing
just like you loved me
the untouchable.
I have spared you myself
and you have gifted me yourself,
for you and I
are no one.

Soldiers Of Love

She was beautiful but she didn't really know.
The transparency of her sincerity has a shade of its own.
Free is the soul when it finds its goal.
No chains of reality can tie it any more,
so blessed is one who was chosen a soldier.
Helping others, "a mission, a faith, an emotion".
So special she was but she didn't know,
The one who has the light doesn't see her own glow.

We Do What We Have To Do

Yes, we move on, we take our souls and fly like spears.
Yes, we delete the feelings and invite the fears.
Yes, we have dreams that life simply smears
and yes, the lips often smile when it quivers with tears.
Yes, we sometimes freeze instead of flee.
Yes, we sometimes delete what we want to keep.
Yes, we sometimes dance when we want to scream,
and yes, yes, we sometimes give our backs
to whom we are dying to see.
We do what we do,
the way we do,
believing it's only what we can do.

"Wish I Wasn't Selfish"

I long for you in the smell of the morning
when the breeze brings to my waking eyes the image of
you.
I long for you when I try to get up from my bed and sit at
the side
to stare at your picture with you still in smiles.
And I know not but to long for you,
when I start to get dressed and I see my image in the
mirror
and almost see you standing there.
And I long for you.
I long for you in the sharpness of noon,
when everyone else is busy making a life.
When the shade starts to appear like a curtain on a stage
pulling in the night.
I long for you,
when people rush to their home,
to the comfort of their family and I am left with the
distance you left deserted.

And I long for you,
when all I hear is the sound of the world sleeping,
yet my eyes stay awake waiting for you to appear from the
darkness.

Then I long for you,
when I finally sink into sleep
expecting you to be there with me,
yet you have departed even from my dreams.
But my body does not comprehend,
it continues to survive like it always did
even though you are not here.
The morning still comes with sunshine
and its yellow rays still fall on my face.
The garden still grows its flowers
and the kids still dance and run chasing happiness with
their tiny legs.
The food is still served with many flavors
and we still feed and grow.
Even the clocks still tick with minutes
that didn't change their pace nor alter their calculation.

And the day, the day is still the twenty-four hours,
not less like it should have been,
everything stayed the same but you.
You left to Him,
HE who loves you more than me.
Yet I selfishly long for you,
wish I wasn't selfish,
but I have loved you more than life will ever see
I have wanted, prayed that what had befallen you had
chosen me.
I wish I wasn't so selfish,
accept that you are in a far better place
but I'm selfish and I long for your face

I am your mommy
you shouldn't beat me in this race
I should have gone first
give me back my place.

Hearts of Light

When I said I love you
A door was open and I stepped in,
weightless, as if I had no sin.
The people there not all of my kin
but a tie stronger than blood was keeping me in.
They all had light shining from their hearts,
some massive, some smaller and some just at its start.
Each admiring the beauty in the heart of the other,
Not aware of their own light.
But light goes to light,
God grants the light.
He, the creator of day and night.
He who blessed the blind with a vision stronger than sight,
He who grants us against our might,
He who guides lost souls to the right,
He who makes peace from a fight,
He who raises seekers of him to heavenly heights,
He who forgive us faster than the speed of light,
He who runs to us when we turn to Him even slight,
He who erases our blackness to white,
He who we'll stand before when life fades to an eternal
night.
May we stand before Him with hearts of light.

Princess and Precious

I stepped towards them
my feet following a hand's wave.
My eyes had not yet seen the faces
but a warmth that the soul chases
was greeting my empty soul.
Then I saw without sight
two creatures of light
too human in their appearance
one named "Princess"
without a crown or a throne
but a smile that twinkled and eyes that glowed.
She and I were buddies in a land of words.
We played together on seesaws of rhythms and prose.
We've flown before with eagles in skies of feelings,
we've rolled together on flower beds.
We've shared the joy of two giggling kids.
We were eternally chosen to be friends.
Even though the years we shared were just in our heads.

Then my eyes spotted the other they call "Precious",
whom I feared to meet
and fear can be vicious,
I had to retreat.
I feared to lose what I was just granted

the key to peek at her from far,
this unique spirit
shining like the Northern Star,
who wants to come close to a wild horse
when its beauty is more visible when you're far, not close?

Why try to approach a blazing sea
when you can gaze from a distance and just let it be
for Precious was precious away from me.
I feared reality would not let her be,
a spirit wild with God's love,
A bold heart similar to none.
They were two,
Princess and Precious.
On one normal morning
so different was their beauty
like night verses day.

But who are they in human words?
I don't really know.
They have stories and memories
that the soul does not show.
The winds of God have placed them before me
and as I sat before them I didn't want to go
for only friendships of the soul
makes the heart grow.

No One But You

If I lose track of myself and stray away
and none of my loved ones behind me stay.
If my footsteps' traces disappear,
if my name is no more but a word they'll hear
and other souls replace my face.
If the grasp of my hand leaves no trace
and people stop asking if I came or left,
If my friends stop looking for me
and my number no longer connects through.
If I become a name on a stone
and flowers no longer grow in lands I own,
if my clothes are worn by other people
and money I earned is not mine any more.
If time has no space or place
and other humans replace this race,
if I become a drop of sand in a galaxy,
and Earth just an extinct space.
Who will search for me in this darkness
But YOU?
Who will blow life into my forgotten soul
But YOU?
Who will find me worthy of a Heaven
but YOU?
This whole world is but a shadow.
There's no truth
but YOU.

My Friend and I

My childhood friend,
how we shared a joke,
at the age of ten.
How birthday gatherings,
were special then.
We were buddies,
he and I,
we shared no similarities,
but together we did laugh and cry.
I always wanted to fly,
and he drew cartoons in the sky.

But I always fancied myself wiser,
for he was months younger than I.
But then we grew,
and things did change,
when I held out my hand,
and he refused to shake.
For a veil had not covered my hair,
and short sleeves were leaving my arms bare.
He gazed away in disapproval,
and walked away.
As another friend volunteered to say,
"Next time when you see him,

no shaking hands!"
Who me? What for?
I failed to comprehend
his logic any more.
And mocked the thought that crossed his mind,
and pitied the days we left behind.

My childhood friend has labeled me among the forbidden,
and developed a language of nods to all women.
Whom had once laughed and talked together,
Kids' games so dear to the heart.
And slowly the drift was a vast shore.
No bridge could bridge it any more.
For my childhood friend and I,
are now enemies in a cold war.

I Found the Bay

I thought I was moving, that my legs had a pace
and my days had a speed,
I thought I had a say to what I do and how I do it.
I thought my voice had a sound
and my eyes could see the light,
I thought I was special, clever,
perhaps even human.
I believed in my power to convince
and my power to believe.
I had faith in people's laughs
and the promise of beauty in their words.
I valued the shine of revenge
in the eyes of the youth.
I fancied how a dancer moves to the rhythms
like the waves move to the winds.
I believed that I knew the secrets of love
even if I never tasted its flavor,
I believed in so much that is so little
and now where am I?
Am I on the other side of the shore?
What am I and who am I?
Am I a mixture that has no color or taste?
Am I walking on a thread in between all what is life
or is it the bridge to all that is after life?

For years I have searched for love
and love escaped me.
It only appeared in shades that my heart could not accept.
The love I searched for was not love.
I have no words to describe it.
I have no mind to define it.
It was a person that is not me
or maybe it is me, if I still lives in me.
I was like a mad man
consumed by the light of his torch
heedless of the light that lies in the darkest night.
Madly believing that he has power
when his power is more false than the truth of a mirage.
Then my time came and he led me to Him.
With every step I took a flower of truthful love bloomed in
my heart.
With every blink of a shining tear,
I felt the touch of love.
And in this very moment I knew the reason of me.
To fall in love.

I know how the heart shakes,
how the lips shiver and the eyes tear at the thought of
one's love.
I know the warmth that is more comforting
than a mother's touch in one's sickness.
I know the support that is more protecting
than a father's back in the midst of crisis.
I know the happiness that is stronger

than the first look at one's own child.
I know the pleasure that is more consuming
than the presence of a lover
after months of absence.
I feel the beauty of nearness
that all the temptations of life cease to exist.

And without learning,
I mastered the secrets of love.
How only in love's weakness to feel wholeness.
I know that if I am with Him I need no one else.
Thinking of Him
is more healing than any medicine ever discovered.
For so long I falsely believed
Love to be a feeling that has limits
but my love for Him grows endlessly
faster than the green seeds He grants life to every second.
I am in love,
in love with THE CREATOR OF LOVE.

I was Young and Wise

Allow me in, this one last time.
I gave you up, without knowing why.
It was one step I took along the way,
that ended with me astray.
Not to sin or ill
but just far away
in a land of boredom
of daily course.
Don't get me wrong
or either way
I did believe, I did pray
but this very heart was always astray.
Does it have to be stung
with death or pride?
Or a game of power
that sweeps like a tide?
Winning and losing,
what made them taste the same?
Was it my ignorance
was it your game?

And the years passed by
without a reason why.
It kept slipping away,

this wisdom of I.
Who said blushing was ever a crime?
Or that innocence
is a fashion out of time,
or a hobby too dumb to be mine?
Well I've mastered emptiness,
if you're looking for wisdom in a face
skip mine.
This heart once held Your faith with pride
and in its depths found rivers of joy
more pleasurable than heaven's wine.
These eyes have wept before Your door
now are lifeless with life's chores.
These lips have whispered, "I love you"
and it has opened Your doors.
But I was young and wise
not old and colored with lies.

I Swear

I swear I can walk to You,
on sea waves I can step through,
on moving waters I can walk too.
I swear I can touch your skies,
ascend to You, miles and miles.
The furthest clouds, I can above them rise.
I swear when I feel Your nearness
the sky and earth collide
and I become fearless.
I swear I can see your angels
in reality not in fables.
We're past friends, not strangers,
I swear.
When I tell You I love You
I am all that
I swear.
When I reach out to You
I become all that.
I become—All that.

Hide Me

I want to run and hide under the fallen leaves
I want to disappear with the wet morning dew,
I want these hands and legs to change into wings
to fly among the birds, unknown.
Hide me.
I want to turn into one of the many waves that wash along
the shores.
I want to become the silence that falls unnoticed on lips
conquered by sleep.
I don't want to step out of the emptiness
and be visible to you
I don't want existence to be my bridge to you.
I don't want to turn into a reality
that poisons the beautiful dreams
I don't want to be a picture and a voice,
I want to be a vision and a dream.
Hide me.

Can you learn to feel the soft breeze of wind
that touches your soul,
without it ever being touched?
Can you learn to see the shadow of an angel
that watches you from afar,
without it ever being watched?

Can you learn to hear the soft murmur of your unborn
child
without it ever being heard?
Can you learn to love me
without being taught?
We met in a moment of pain
two people lost on the end of a rainbow
where color and paleness are one shade,
where night and day are one and the same
where truth and lies are but a game.
We met as strangers and talked as strangers
and dreamt as strangers.
Each of us was on a different road,
till our souls met.

Suddenly I noticed that gardens grow roses along with
cactuses
I noticed that the night is not so dark,
for little stars wave at us from afar.
I noticed that the cold rain is not so cruel
for young children dance with pleasure under its showers.
I noticed that sharing feelings isn't a crime
for even flowers bloom when they feel loved.
I noticed that life could be mine.
Hide me.
I never asked you to join me
and you never invited me to follow you,
like we both feared to voice what we longed for
that life would slash the dream.
It's like we couldn't breathe a word,
that the words would turn into tears.

It's like we both knew love words must not be spoken,
or they would morph into fears.
And the moment of sharing was gone
each of us continued on his own way home,
Like two blind people who saw each other for a moment,
but couldn't say
alas the passion of sharing would be gone.
I want to stay blind,
never to see you and never to be seen by you.
I want to remain silent,
never to speak and never to be heard by you.
For you found me and I found you.
in a moment of blindness.
Hide me.

I'll Kill You

I decided to kill you. To kill me.
I decided to shut my doors,
block out every window on my walls.
I decided to poison everything and anything
I decided to talk, to confess, to claim myself the butcher.
I decided to face the winds of my feelings
To release them outside my heart,
to name them my enemies.
I decided to combat the softness in my voice,
to chain these lips that learnt to speak of love to you.
I decided to tell you "no"
tell you "go, go."
I decided I can't love,
won't love,
shouldn't love.

I decided that my heart is not to be a witness in this.
I decided to speak out to you.
To tell you with all the love I love you,
I can't love.
Then run away from your gaze
Before I once more melt in you.
My love is your enemy
the storm you can't live through,
don't give in to feelings,
my love will brutally kill you.

Me and I

In the distance of warmth
I have befriended my own self,
we have secretly
talked, laughed and walked down colorful woods
and we have shared old stories of people
who once were with us
and now are gone.

The Sun Shines at Midnight

Take me with you to a land that smiles day and night
take me further than the last ray of light
I will laugh so loud
I'll replace the crowd
I'll undo my hair
I'll chase butterflies everywhere
I'll copy the sound of the wind
the flying petals I'll befriend
I'll draw circles in the sand
I'll stand on one hand
I'll stuff my mouth with chewing gum
I'll stick out my tongue
I'll change my name to "Sunshine"
I'll sip my juice and pretend it's wine
and before the sun goes down,
I'll carve these words on this black ground,
"THIS DARKNESS HAS SUNSHINE."

Little Soul

Feel brave, little soul
the signal you're hearing
is truly your call,
trust your heart
don't let it fall apart,
your mind may not see it
but your inside feels it
you were meant to know
what your eyes never saw,
the message was clear
there's nothing to fear
you may think you're alone
but He is forever near.

Love's Recipe

HE made it with a recipe
of magic and wonder
and spiced it with dreams,
euphoria and a strike like thunder.
Then HE named it love
and blessed all His creations with its splendor,
but HE didn't teach the birds
to love the fluff of their wings across the skies,
HE didn't teach the petals
to lovingly greet the dew before sunrise,
HE didn't teach the heart
to love blindly without eyes.
For HE who created love
created it for the mindless and the wise.

While Mom Sleeps

I stare at her long
As she sleeps in her bed
Wondering what news pleased her most
From all the things I said
Was it how her grandchildren
Had nailed the best grades
Or my success delighted her most
admiring all my traits
or was it the touch of my brother's hand
that lit her heart
when life was too much to stand
I thought of her sweet smile
that assures me that all's fine
I thought of how her morning tea waits
till she serves me mine
I thought of the cheese sandwich she loves
she'd even have it for lunch
Past the decades
Never changed much
I stare at her long
Before she wakes up
Even the few hours she sleeps
In her absence is too much.

A Fable

There's a weakness in my heart
that only you can fill
there's a bleeding spot
that's leaking still
I thought it had gone dry
When my heart
ceased to cry
I thought its flowers wilted
when the ground beneath me
no longer tilted
I thought I was through thorough and stable
I thought wrong
forgetting you is a fable.

Made of Deeds

I am of no face, of no features
I am the heart that acted kindly
and the tongue that hurt brutally,
I am the good I did
and the good I wrecked
I am made of my deeds
the virtuous and the wicked
they all appear
no make-up could conceal.

Tell Them She Will Love Me

Tell them she will love me,
Till autumn stops shedding its leaves
The yellow shades can color every tree
But her absence constantly grieves.
Tell them she will love me,
Till summer abandons its hot air
The sunlight can cover up the world
But her absence leaves the soul bare.
Tell them she will love me,
Till spring no longer blooms
The flowers can dazzle lovers
But her absence smoothly dooms.
Tell them she will love me
Till winter is a word unknown
The snow can soften the world
But her absence turns me to stone.

Rich

I wish feelings were sold
I'd sell all my gold
And buy bundles of joy,
containers of laugher
And buckets of happiness.
I'd fill my cupboards
With good wishes
I'd grow smiles
In deserted bushes.
I'd save in my safe box
piles of delight
I might then be rich,
I just might.

What If I Grow Old?

What if I grow old
but not with age,
Regardless of the lines
that shape counters of my face,
Oblivious of the thoughts
and feelings that rage,
So long as the soul is freed
of any cage.

What if I grow old
but not with years,
With the charm of laughs
that churned the tears,
And fears that perished
before the dreams,
In hasty days
that grew into years.

What if I grow old
but much in vain,
With losses forgotten
before any gain.
The sweeter the memory

the greater the pain
And acceptance that nothing lasts,
Not even the greatest fame.

What if I grow old
but yet so bold,
Never accepting a life
labeled cold,
Never following the crowd
and whatever is told,
Never a fake imitation
or a lifeless mold.

What if I grow old
faster than my years,
With a heart that conquers
All the frightening fears,
And feet that step
on a thousand piers,
Yet always ready to depart
without any tears,
Who wants to linger
in temporary dreams,
When YOUR eternal heavens
are built on streams?

Either, Or

When gone people will either tell
She was of a good will
Or her deeds were so ill
they'll either label me a saint
Or a demon at hell's gate
they'll count me among the pious
Or a seeker of deadly chaos
I'll either be a "matter" to be told
Or a "nothingness"
like mist in the cold.
Who cares?
If Heaven is where
my story will be told.

Anywhere

Far from here
Far from everything there
Far to the other side
Far where our dreams hide
Where kites disappear
Far in that place
Where youth vanishes
And every love song was first created
Further than feet can walk
Further than planes can reach
Further than the eyes can see.
Far is distance and far in space
From where you were created
Before you were a dot in a womb
Before a voice was given a sound
Before the eyes were granted a sight
Far from who you are
Far from where you are
Far from what you are meant to be

Who We Are

We are one and all.
The master and the slave,
the prisoner and the jury,
the innocent and the villain.
One and all.
Just roles we play,
changing continuously.
Just dreams we slay,
fading casually.

You Are Alive

You are alive
In the heavenly sound of music
More clear in the twinkle
of the hearty tear
You are alive in the breath of this pigeon
That spoke of your love before the beginning of time
You are alive in the ray of light that chose to make of this
morning a day.
You are alive in the reaction of their faces when happiness and
sorrow combine

I Want Just Me

Stop the minutes,
Halt the hours, I long for my haven,
Where I am just me.
Where curly hair and sand blend so free,
Where no makeup is worn,
And no fancy dress is searched for,
Where humanly matters cease to exist any more,
Where only God's light reflects onto the soul.

No Escape from Me

I am not the face of you
I am layers of he and she
I'm a tree inside your heart
I am a bird that won't depart
I am the blackness that morphed into light
I am all the images of you
The unspoken
And the spoken too

Mobile Slave

Unchain me, I've become your slave
I imprisoned myself willingly in your cage
I've abandoned sun's rays of light
For your fake, artificial light
I've surrounded myself with smiles
That never possessed a life.
In your world
my voice echoes back,
In your world
Even a so-called friend can hack.
And when we lie and when we cheat
And when colored facts
Be the language we speak
And I dissolve in you
And you become a part of me
I stare at your mightiness
In the grasp of my hand
And wonder if I can ever escape your land
A human finger obsessed by a never-ending game
Of a tomorrow that will be live
Through a five-inch screen
And a reality that has been hacked
By a computerized, synchronized dream.